Victor Hugo's Wondrous Feast

The Tabernacle Choir at Temple Square provides artistic expressions of faith from The Church of Jesus Christ of Latter-day Saints.

Historical photographs courtesy of Priaulx Library (priaulxlibrary.co.uk).

Lesley Nicol photographs by Hunter Winterton and Leslie Nilsson. Photograph of The Tabernacle Choir by Ron Crapo. Used by permission.

© 2024 Intellectual Reserve, Inc.

Text © 2024 Intellectual Reserve, Inc.

Paintings © 2024 David T. Warner

All rights reserved. No part of this book may be reproduced in any form or by any means without permission in writing from the publisher, Shadow Mountain Publishing®, at permissions@shadowmountain.com. The views expressed herein are the responsibility of the authors and do not necessarily represent the position of Shadow Mountain Publishing.

Visit us at shadowmountain.com. Visit the Choir at TheTabernacleChoir.org.

Library of Congress Cataloging-in-Publication Data

(CIP data on file)

ISBN 978-1-63993-324-2

Printed in the United States of America
Phoenix Color Corporation, Hagerstown, MD   7/2024

10 9 8 7 6 5 4 3 2 1

Victor Hugo's Wondrous Feast

The True Story of How the Author of Les Misérables Inspired the World to Love

WITH INTRODUCTION BY
LESLEY NICOL

AS PERFORMED BY
THE TABERNACLE CHOIR AT TEMPLE SQUARE

WRITTEN AND ILLUSTRATED BY
DAVID T. WARNER

SHADOW
MOUNTAIN
PUBLISHING

INTRODUCTION BY LESLEY NICOL

I had the privilege of narrating this true story as part of the annual Christmas concert of The Tabernacle Choir and Orchestra at Temple Square. Accompanied by an orchestral underscore, two French carols, and a cast of supporting actors, this rendition was seen by a live audience of over 50,000 and recorded for broadcast on PBS. That's quite a reach for an intimate story about a few people in the Channel Islands. And yet it's a story that can bless the world.

It certainly blessed me. Throughout the production week, my agent, Paul Pearson, and I marveled at how 400-plus volunteer musicians, artisans, and crew members worked together in a spirit of mutual respect, cooperation, and, frankly, love. Truly, they embodied the story's theme To Love Is to Act. In my role as an actor, I was able to embrace that theme simply by doing my part—by acting. Through it all, I was reminded that it is impossible to give of ourselves at Christmastime without receiving more in return. What did I receive? A few minutes before the story portion of the concert, the Choir joined Broadway performer Michael Maliakel in singing "Have Yourself a Merry Little Christmas." The first verse of that song includes the simple invitation: "Let your heart be light." That's what happened to me, my fellow performers, and audience members. Our hearts became light, even joyful, nourished by a wondrous feast of Christmas music and messages.

As the story came to an end, I repeated the powerful phrase "Aimer c'est agir," or in English, "to love is to act." Those were practically the last words written by Victor Hugo before he died. But for us, during a few special days with the Tabernacle Choir, they became words to live by. May they also inspire you to live, to actively love, and to "let your heart be light."

Lesley

Victor Hugo loved life. Born in France in 1802, he was still a boy when he discovered that he could use words to express his love for people, ideas, and causes. He also learned that he could inspire readers to do hard things, including helping people in need regardless of their backgrounds and beliefs. And since that is the most courageous kind of love, Victor knew that he had an important work to do.

When he was just ten years old, Victor wrote his first play. Five years later, the prestigious French Academy awarded one of his poems honorable mention, even though the judges did not believe such a young person had written it. At the age of twenty, he published his first book and married his childhood friend, Adèle Foucher.

Victor and Adèle's family grew quickly, and so did their love for their children. At night, Victor told them stories and left little drawings on their pillows. He believed that all children come from God, and he wrote about them with love and respect.

And how he wrote—page after page after page! The more that people read his stories, poems, and plays, the more they were inspired by his descriptions of love—forgiving enemies, feeding the poor, befriending the lonely, and protecting the weak.

Victor himself aspired to love in this active way. In 1851, when a new emperor diminished freedoms and disregarded the poor, Victor's love for France and her people prompted him to speak up. This angered the government. So, for safety, the Hugos moved to Belgium and then to the Channel Islands. But living in exile—far away from home and friends—was not easy for Victor and Adèle or for their grown children.

Eventually, the Hugos settled on the island of Guernsey. There Victor bought Hauteville House, a three-story mansion perched on a hill overlooking the town of St. Peter Port.

One morning, Adèle went to market. She was used to passing all kinds of people on the street. But that day, what she saw touched her heart and filled her with a special kind of love. Standing in the sunlight was a five-year-old girl holding a small child. The younger one was crying for her mother. They had no coats, no shoes, and no one to look after them.

When Adèle returned home, she told Victor, "I cannot get their faces from my mind. I imagine our own children standing there with nothing to eat and nowhere to go."

"Ah!" Victor exclaimed. "The light of conscience is not easy to put out!" For Victor, that light was the quiet voice in all of us—a feeling that we should act, even though it may not be easy. "So," he asked Adèle, "what will we do to help those poor children?"

At first, Adèle wrote to newspapers to raise funds for a day care. But the money she received was not enough, so she gave it to local charities. She also made swaddling blankets to help needy mothers wrap their newborn babies.

Meanwhile, from his writing room overlooking the ocean, Victor was finishing his most famous story, *Les Misérables*, or in English, *The Wretched Ones*. Readers would come to love many characters in that book, including several children in need—dear little Cosette, brave Gavroche, and his heroic older sister, Éponine.

They may have been on Victor's mind when he read an interesting medical report. Doctors had discovered that many childhood diseases could be prevented if children ate better food, including at least one balanced meal each month. So, led by the light of conscience, Victor and Adèle made a plan.

In March 1862, Adèle announced to their servants, "We have decided to invite the poorest children in Guernsey for a weekly dinner with us here in Hauteville House." Adèle told the cook, "I want the children to have the finest meal possible. Only the best cuts of beef. No scraps!"

But their son Charles did not like the idea. "What? Inside our house? They are urchins and beggars, with bugs in their hair and dirt on their clothes. And they don't smell nice!"

But Victor and Adèle were determined to look beyond outward appearances. "The dinners should be open to children of all nationalities, backgrounds, and religions," Victor directed. "If there are vacant places, admit the poorest children first."

Later, he explained his special feeling for these young guests. "They, too, are outcasts," he wrote, "exiled from all enjoyment and happiness."

In the beginning, the Hugos arranged for eight children to attend the dinners, then fifteen, then thirty-two. Soon there were two groups rotating every other week, including a few mothers.

Once through the tall front doors, the children freely explored the richly appointed house, each room a reminder that a great author named Victor Hugo knew them and welcomed them in.

A few months later, the Hugos hosted forty children for an elaborate Christmas celebration. Victor also invited journalists, artists, priests, and other dignitaries, hoping they would write about their experiences and inspire similar dinners around the world.

When these grown-up visitors arrived, Victor explained to them, "Dear friends, what we are doing here in our home, all of us have a responsibility to do. So, we ask you to join us—come, help, serve!"

With that encouragement, all rolled up their sleeves to wait on the children, serve them food, and present them with gifts.

Victor's plan worked. The visitors reported what they saw and felt in newspaper editorials, articles, and letters:

"The children entered happily, without shyness, as if it were their own home!"

"Though the children were poor and wretched, the Hugos received them with open arms."

"Gifts of clothing are laid out on the billiard table, and there is a Christmas tree with toys and presents just for them."

"Mr. Hugo gathered the children around him: 'You are my little brothers and sisters in the good Lord,' he said. 'You do not owe me anything, but you should be grateful to God, the Father of us all. If you want to thank anyone for it, it should be Him.'"

After the eldest child offered prayer, all partook of the sumptuous meal. Joyfully, they slurped soup, savored roast beef, and gobbled pastries, pies, and puddings. But they devoured more than food. They feasted on love.

As Victor hoped, word of the dinners spread. Similar efforts were undertaken for impoverished children in Britain, Europe, South America, the Caribbean, and the United States. In one London parish, 6,000 children enjoyed a banquet inspired by the Hugos' wondrous Christmas feast.

And wondrous it was. But the wonder was not so much in the food as in the feeling. People of varied ages and backgrounds filled the Hugos' home with laughter and conversation. Notwithstanding their different cultures, religious denominations, and economic backgrounds, they sat side by side. Feasting together made them one.

For seven more years, as long as the Hugos lived in Guernsey, children came weekly to Hauteville House for a meal. Victor and Adèle spent one-third of their household budget to buy the food and prepare it. Victor also wrote about what he called "the rights of the child," advocating that children be protected, healthy, and happy.

Why did the Hugos do so much to bless little ones? The answer can be found in three words Victor wrote just before he died: "Aimer c'est agir," which in English means "to love is to act." It is a theme, a golden thread, running through all his work.

Aimer c'est agir
Victor Hugo

Victor's work was not just *writing* about love, it was also about *inspiring* people to love in an active way—the way taught by a Light greater than Victor himself. He explained to his adult visitors, "Has not the Lord said, 'Suffer the children to come unto me'? I desire that this invitation be universally accepted. It is not just a charitable meal for needy children. It is a way to foster brotherhood, sow seeds of human solidarity, and make peace."

Victor Hugo did love life. When he died, he left behind over fifty published works affirming that everyone can love others, including those who may be very different from us. Whether painting a picture, baking a pie, or fixing a pipe, to love is to act—to do whatever we can to help a person in need.

When that is our aim, we are not content to remain at a distance. We willingly open ourselves to know, understand, and serve the people around us, whoever they may be. Loving in this way, we see the true light in one another, even the face of God.

And that is the most wondrous feast of all.

AFTERWORD
The Transformational Work of Love

Image courtesy of The Priaulx Library, Guernsey

In early March 1862, Victor and Adèle Hugo held their first dinner for a few wretched, poorly nourished children on the Isle of Guernsey. It is impossible to know the extent of the children's deprivation, but the nature of Victorian society tells us they never expected to walk through the doors of the Hugos' opulent house or enjoy a sumptuous meal at their table.

The Hugos did know, however, the effect that such an experience could have on their young guests. In less than a month, Victor's masterpiece *Les Misérables* would be released in Paris and sell out within twenty-four hours. As readers eagerly opened that book, they encountered this unforgettable scenario:

A wretched, starving ex-convict is invited into the humble house of a Catholic bishop and enjoys a simple meal at the bishop's table—a meal that was sumptuous by prison standards. That night, terrified by the uncertainty of his future and embittered by his own unjust imprisonment, the man steals the bishop's silver and runs. When he's captured with the stolen property, he's astonished by what the bishop tells the police: "I'm sure this man told you the silver was given to him by an old priest. It's true." Then, turning to the ex-convict, he warmly chides, "Dear friend, you left behind your silver candlesticks! Don't forget to take them, too!"

At that moment, the ex-convict is forever changed. He is not only rescued from a terrible fate, he is also redeemed by love. It's not the meal that transforms him. It is the bishop's mercy, brotherhood, and willingness to bear his suffering with him.

And that is exactly what the Hugos' dinners were about. Some might read them as a welfare project or public health program. But in fact, they were an act of love by two people who knew very well how mercy, kindness, and compassion could alter one's future and transform one's soul. That was their goal for the children of Guernsey. Here are some of the ways they accomplished it:

They held the dinners in their home, where the children entered without timidity and were encouraged to be themselves. "I was present at one of these dinners," L. H. Toulzanne wrote in his book *A Week in Guernsey*. "I found observing [the meal] both touching and charming, and really moving. . . . The little diners sparkled with . . . mischief and childish fun."

The Hugos knew the children's names and provided Christmas gifts selected for them. The record of one Christmas feast includes: "There were boots for ten-year-old Clémence Philippe" and "a dress for nine-year-old Virginie Etasse."

Victor also took the opportunity to teach the children on a variety of subjects, including the importance of work and preparing for an occupation. One Christmas, after distributing gifts around the tree, he told the children, "Among the toys I have just given you, you will find no guns, no cannon or swords, no murderous weapon that could make you think of war or destruction. War is a dreadful thing. The people of the world are made for loving one another."

Victor was specifically not interested in "indulging in the luxury of mitigating misery," as one newspaper article reported. Relieving suffering was not enough. The Hugos wanted to promote flourishing.

That flourishing included fraternity with the world—a sense of brotherhood and sisterhood among all people. "The children eat together, all as one, Catholics, Protestants, English, French, Irish, whatever religion or nationality they may be." Victor said the same about their adult guests: "Catholic priests and Protestant ministers [mingle] with free-thinking liberals . . . , and I don't think any leave unhappy."

Above all, Victor wanted the children to understand that God is the source of every blessing—blessings they could continue to receive after the dinners were over. One journalist reported him saying, "Your thanks are due not to me, but to God, the giver of all good." Similarly, in *Les Misérables*, the bishop assures the poor ex-convict: "This is not my house, it is the house of Jesus Christ. If you suffer, if you are hungry and thirsty, you are welcome here. Do not thank me. . . . Everything here is yours."

In the spring of 1862, the Hugos were living out the story Victor had just written—a story that would eventually be translated into over 20 languages and retold in visual art, plays, films, and the beloved musical known as *Les Mis*. Victor knew that in the sweep of the entire novel, the bishop's role seemed relatively small. But the man he helped did not remain a wretched, starving ex-convict. He became Jean Valjean, the hero who would go on to save souls in the fictional narrative and inspire the world for generations to come. That's the transformational work of love. It is work all of us can do—work that goes on forever.

Research for this essay was drawn from the thoughtful work of Dinah Bott, chair of The Victor Hugo in Guernsey Society (victorhugoinguernsey.gg), and Dr. Marva A. Barnett, author and professor emerita at the University of Virginia. For more information, see Ms. Bott's articles "My Little Brothers: Christmas with Victor Hugo, 1862" and "Victor Hugo's Christmas Fete, 1865" (published at priaulxlibrary.co.uk) and Dr. Barnett's most recent book, *To Love Is to Act:* Les Misérables *and Victor Hugo's Vision for Leading Lives of Conscience* (Swan Isle Press, 2020). Special thanks to Ms. Bott and Dr. Barnett for ongoing consultation and to The Priaulx Library in Guernsey, Channel Islands, for granting access to source materials. Grateful acknowledgment is given to Alexandra MacKenzie-Johns for her invaluable collaboration in creating The Tabernacle Choir presentation on which this book is based.

CHRISTMAS WITH THE TABERNACLE CHOIR

For more than twenty years, Christmas lovers around the world have looked forward to the latest broadcast of *Christmas with the Tabernacle Choir*—the annual holiday concert of The Tabernacle Choir and Orchestra at Temple Square. Each December in the Conference Center of The Church of Jesus Christ of Latter-day Saints, these concerts thrill live audiences of more than 60,000. But across the world, millions watch them on PBS through the Choir's partnership with GBH and BYU Television and through select excerpts on the Choir's popular social channels.

As host, the internationally renowned Choir and Orchestra are pleased to feature solo artists from stage, screen, and television. These include Broadway singers and actors Alfie Boe, Kristin Chenoweth, Santino Fontana, Sutton Foster, Megan Hilty, Angela Lansbury, Michael Maliakel, Brian Stokes Mitchell, Kelli O'Hara, Laura Osnes, and Lea Salonga; opera stars Renée Fleming, Nathan Gunn, Frederica von Stade, Bryn Terfel, Rolando Villazón, and Deborah Voight; Grammy Award–winner Natalie Cole, *American Idol* finalist David Archuleta; and The Muppets® from *Sesame Street*®. The concerts have also welcomed acclaimed actors Claire Bloom, Hugh Bonneville, Peter Graves, Edward Herrmann, Martin Jarvis, Neal McDonough, Lesley Nicol, John Rhys-Davies, Jane Seymour, Sir David Suchet, Richard Thomas, and Michael York; famed broadcast journalist Tom Brokaw, Pulitzer Prize–winning author David McCullough, and noted TV news anchorman Walter Cronkite.

At the heart of the celebration are 360 Choir members and a roster of more than 200 Orchestra members. These unpaid volunteers are men and women from many countries, backgrounds, and professions who perform more than 50 times each year in live concerts, broadcasts, recordings, and world tours. In major performances, they are often joined by The Bells at Temple Square, a thirty-two-member handbell choir. Together these musicians are dedicated to the mission of sharing inspired music throughout the world—music that has the power to heal, comfort, strengthen, and bring people closer to the divine.

Among its many performances, The Tabernacle Choir's weekly *Music & the Spoken Word* program is the longest-running continuous broadcast in history and includes Spanish and Portuguese versions with voice-over translation in other languages. Five of the Choir's recordings have achieved "gold record" and two have achieved "platinum record" status. Its recordings have reached the #1 position on *Billboard*® magazine's classical lists a remarkable fifteen times since 2003. Today, music from the Choir and Orchestra is available through the Choir's YouTube channel, Spotify, Apple Music, Amazon Music, and Pandora.

To watch the broadcast performance of the story in this book, featuring Lesley Nicol, Michael Maliakel, the Choir, and Orchestra, please visit TabChoir.org/VictorHugo.